D0996928

AN INTRODUCTION TO
BONSAI

盆栽

AN INTRODUCTION TO
BONSAI

BY THE BONSAI KAI OF THE JAPAN SOCIETY

TIGER BOOKS INTERNATIONAL
LONDON

This edition published in 1989 by
Tiger Books International PLC, London.

ISBN 1-870461-86-X

Produced by Ward Lock Ltd, London

Text © Bonsai Kai, London 1989
Illustrations © Dandelion Editions Ltd 1989

The publishers are grateful to Peter Adams,
Dan Barton, Peter Chan, Bill Jordan, Colin
Lewis, James McCurrach and Harry
Tomlinson for permission to use
photographs of their trees in this book.

Printed in Italy

CONTENTS

WHAT IS A BONSAI?

A bonsai is a tree or other plant, or a group of trees or plants, cultivated in a container. The meaning of the word is 'plant in a pot'. The growing of bonsai began long ago in China, but for perhaps a thousand years it has been practised and perfected as an art in Japan. The art is in choosing a plant which has the potential to become a good bonsai, and then growing it with skill so that it blends with its container to form an impression of nature in miniature. The difference between bonsai and other potted plants is that the beauty of the bonsai is the beauty of the whole composition, the balance and harmony of tree and pot. A bonsai may be only a few inches tall yet may still give the impression of a towering tree on a hillside or of a pine clinging to a windswept cliff's edge. But perfection is rare and enjoyment does not depend upon it.

Bonsai are variously bought, grown from seed, collected from nature, grafted, layered and divided. The aim is to own and cultivate a plant which though small in size has the appearance of being seasoned, matured and in certain cases aged.

TWIN TRUNK EUROPEAN LARCH

(Larix decidua)

Two matchstick-thick seedlings were planted side by side in 1974 to start this impressive and unusual bonsai. This style evokes memories of lone trees standing high on a distant hill, with the numerous jins (dead, stripped branches) telling how it alone has survived while all the surrounding trees have perished. Although it is only 26 inches tall it creates an illusion of immense height.

BEGINNING A BONSAI COLLECTION

Without doubt the easiest way to begin is by buying a bonsai. It should already be clear that buying a bonsai means buying the grower's time and effort, perhaps over many years; good bonsai are therefore expensive. There is great satisfaction in owning a fine specimen, perhaps to be used as a yardstick against which to judge one's own efforts in future. However a specimen tree requires attention throughout the year just like any other bonsai and the beginner may be wary, and rightly so, of learning the various techniques on his prize possession. If beginning a collection with an expensive purchase it is advisable to make friends rapidly with an experienced bonsai enthusiast or join a club or society to get advice, particularly during the first year.

Many excellent potential bonsai can be obtained from a garden centre or nursery. Young plants are relatively cheap, and interesting shapes which will make good bonsai are often shunned by the ordinary gardener. Sometimes the nurseryman may even be glad to have them taken off his hands at a reduced price. The potential bonsai should of course be healthy and preferably have a good thick trunk. When grown in a container in a nursery the trunk is often hidden below the soil level. A thick trunk and good top growth generally indicate good roots and this combination provides the soundest starting point for good bonsai. Container trees of course can be bought at any time of the year and kept until the appropriate time to begin training. Trees grown in the ground will have to be accepted for delivery at the normal time and heeled into the garden to await the right time of year for potting.

Many of the very best bonsai have been found in the wild, high up in the mountains, on cliffs or on the seashore. But these may only be collected with the consent of the landowner, which is often

TWIN TRUNK, DRIFTWOOD STYLE NEEDLE JUNIPER
(Juniperus rigida)
This most impressive tree, with its masses of dramatic driftwood, was reputed to be 98 years old when it was imported in 1979. The form and mass of the lower trunk provide a perfect foil to the 29 inch tall main trunk.

difficult to obtain. The shape of the trunk is of paramount importance because, being old wood, it cannot be greatly altered. The branches are often poor but this should not discourage the collector because new branches can be encouraged to grow by pruning.

The best season for collecting is in early spring before the new buds open. It is important to collect as much of the root of the tree as possible but in general terms the top of the tree should be pruned in proportion to the root ball. In early spring root growth is at its fastest. Nevertheless it is usually advisable to plant a new acquisition in open ground for up to three years to regenerate new roots before it is potted. An alternative is to prune the roots in its natural home a year or more before final collection. Wild seedlings can also be collected and trained, being especially suitable for group plantings.

It goes without saying that the collector should abide by the law and seek the necessary permission for his activities. After being replanted, all trees collected in the wild should be protected from direct sun and wind, and the earth and surrounding atmosphere should be kept moist until the trees have overcome the shock of transplantation. If the tree is in good condition strong new buds will appear on the branches in due course.

Plants of any species may be grown from seed for training as bonsai, though of course this method is the slowest. For the best results fresh seed sown immediately after collection in the autumn is advised. Normal seed sowing procedures are used. Pine seedlings should be left undisturbed for a year but deciduous seedlings can be transplanted after about six months. Seedlings will grow more quickly in the open ground than in pots.

Many trees, with the notable exception of pines, can be propagated from cuttings. The cuttings are taken in the same way as for ordinary full-sized trees. It is generally accepted that there are two seasons for taking cuttings: early spring just as new buds are beginning to grow and late summer when the last growth is being made.

立木

INFORMAL STYLE RED HAWTHORN
(Crataegus cuneata)
Imported from Japan in 1975, this beautiful flowering hawthorn seems more ancient than its 50 years. The neat foliage, delightful blossom, bright red fruit and well-formed branch structure make this truly a tree for all seasons. It is currently 20 inches tall.

However experienced gardeners will know that these are rules that can frequently be broken. Sustained new growth will indicate a successful 'take'. At the end of six to 12 months, depending upon the species, the cutting may be transplanted into a training pot or, as with seedlings, into the open ground if more rapid growth is required.

Trees that allow you to take cuttings easily often throw up plenty of suckers. Elm, birch and lilac all produce suckers and you can often get a good potential bonsai with roots already growing by taking a suitable sucker. However if you have to dig too deep for the roots the result is likely to be an unsatisfactory and leggy tree.

As a general rule first quality bonsai can never be created by grafting unless much effort over many years is expended to erase the signs of the graft. As with all general rules there are exceptions but grafting is in any case a relatively complicated procedure, which is not recommended to the beginner in bonsai growing.

Layering and dividing, which follow normal garden practice, are also useful techniques for creating bonsai.

INFORMAL UPRIGHT SCOTS PINE
(Pinus sylvestris)
This highly individually styled yet convincing tree was created by Peter Adams from collected material. Its mature flakey bark and the severe bends in the trunk give this tree a natural craggy appearance which would be impossible to produce using nursery-grown stock. Its age is estimated to be around 60 years.

PETER ADAMS

SUITABLE BONSAI MATERIAL

The techniques of growing bonsai reduce the size of the leaves compared with those of a tree grown in open ground. However, trees with naturally very large leaves do not as a rule reduce their leaf size sufficiently for the leaves to be in proportion to the size of the bonsai. Moreover although leaf size is reduced by growing the tree as a bonsai, generally neither flower nor fruit size is reduced. Thus certain plants are aesthetically unsuitable as bonsai unless the grower is unconcerned by these disproportions. Few conifers present this problem but of the broad leaved tree the field maple, for example, is more suitable than the sycamore and the white poplar than the black Italian poplar. However where the leaf is compound, as in mountain ash for example, the eye is deceived into regarding the small leaflets as leaves and for this reason many trees with compound leaves make very attractive bonsai. As was said earlier, bonsai is an art in which one seeks to create an impression. It follows that the most successful flowering and fruiting bonsai have naturally small flowers and fruits; cotoneaster, pyracantha and hawthorn are examples with these desirable features. Moreover all these have naturally small leaves.

FORMAL UPRIGHT NEEDLE JUNIPER
(Juniperus rigida)
The most striking feature of this 90 year old juniper is the unusual 'shari' (exposed heartwood) which runs the entire length of the trunk. At 35 inches tall, this is a deceptively large tree.

CLASSIC BONSAI STYLES

娑羅幹

Sharimiki — Driftwood style

懸崖

Kengai — Cascade style

直幹

Chokkan — Formal upright style

立木

Tachiki — Informal upright style

Netsunagari — Sinuous raft style 根連

Han-kengai — Semi-cascade style 半懸崖

Sabamiki — Split-trunk style 姿婆幹

Sôju — Twin trunk style 雙樹

Fukinagashi — Windswept style 吹流

Kabudachi — Clump style 株立

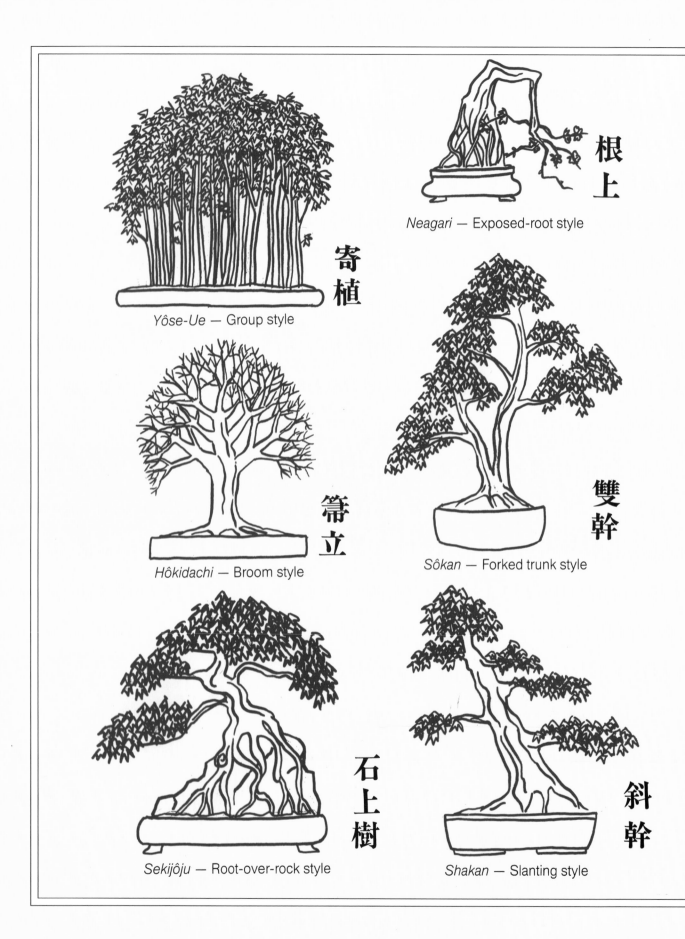

寄植
Yôse-Ue — Group style

根上
Neagari — Exposed-root style

箒立
Hôkidachi — Broom style

雙幹
Sôkan — Forked trunk style

石上樹
Sekijôju — Root-over-rock style

斜幹
Shakan — Slanting style

筏吹

Ikadabuki — Straight-line raft style

三本寄

Sambon-Yôse — Triple-trunk style

文人木

Bunjingi — Literati style

蛸造

Takozukuri — Octopus style

蟠幹

Bankan — Twisted style

石付

Ishitsuki — Root-on-rock style

CARE AND ATTENTION

A small tree in a small pot needs to be looked after. When and how are outlined in the next few pages and in the work schedule. The aim of growing bonsai is not miniaturisation alone, but the end product of cultivating a healthy and well proportioned tree using appropriate training techniques. Healthy but controlled growth is required. To be healthy the tree needs adequate feeding and sufficient air and water; thus the bonsai is not deprived for the purpose of dwarfing. Nor is there any chemical dwarfing agent applied to bonsai. It is well to remember that when a plant stops growing it begins dying and some bonsai alive today are recorded as being over 400 years old.

Any person who wishes to grow bonsai should spare at least ten to 20 minutes every day to the task. Without such effort successful bonsai growing can hardly be expected. However even a city flat dweller with no previous experience of gardening can grow bonsai successfully provided there is a convenient window box or balcony for the trees to live on. Most bonsai are hardy and must live out of doors. They should rarely be brought indoors for more than 24 hours at a time.

GROUP STYLE SPRUCE
(Picea glehnii)
The tallest tree in this group is 36 inches and is about 40 years old. Originally imported in the early 60s, it has undergone inevitable changes but has always retained its charm. The tiny fungi growing in the pot are natural, and their presence is an indication that the trees are in good health. They help to break down the nutrients in the soil, making these easier for the tree to absorb.

In contrast to the non-gardening flat dweller, those who are accustomed to growing plants will find that the techniques of growing bonsai are largely based on good garden practice.

In general a bonsai will take longer to come to maturity than it would if grown in open ground. If well cared for and protected it may well out-live an ordinary tree. Not all trees are equally slow in growing, and trees which begin as cut-tings or layerings — or, faster yet, as small and untrained promising nursery trees from a garden centre — have a good start over trees grown from seed. In certain circumstances trees grown in open ground may provide an even better start. A very acceptable bonsai can be created in about three years and give a great deal of enjoyment in that time as well as much subsequent satisfac-tion. The chief beauty of the bonsai is the impres-sion of maturity which can be created in a rela-tively young plant given the right species, speci-men and skills. Even from seed a very pleasing larch or maple bonsai can be produced in a few years.

COLIN LEWIS

INFORMAL UPRIGHT STYLE WHEATLEY ELM
(Ulmus carpinifolia wheatleyi)
At only eleven years old this tree conveys the feeling of maturity with its strong trunk line and well-positioned branches. It was developed from a self-sown seedling and now stands at 12 inches tall.

寄
植

GROUP STYLE CRYPTOMERIA
(Cryptomeria japonica 'Yatsubutsa')
This planting had only been a bonsai in the
true sense for about eighteen months
when this photograph was taken. The
lifelike impression of a forest glade was
achieved by using plants of different ages
and thicknesses to give perspective. The
oldest tree is ten years old and the
youngest only six.

HARRY TOMLINSON

POTTING, REPOTTING AND ROOT PRUNING

Bonsai exist only in containers; it is a combination of growing in the container and training that makes the bonsai. A healthy bonsai puts out new roots every year and these make it increasingly difficult for water and air to penetrate the soil. The plant will therefore become pot bound and regeneration of the roots will slow down and eventually stop unless the roots are cut back from time to time. How often this is done depends on the tree's rate of growth. Evergreens may only require root pruning once every three or four years; some deciduous trees once every two or three years; very quick growing trees every year. The best season for repotting is in early spring up to the time when the first buds break.

Certain flowering trees, e.g. quince, are an exception and should be repotted immediately after flowering, but in general the idea is to root prune at a time when new root growth will be rapid and also when the tree has not made any new top growth. If root pruning when the tree is in full growth is unavoidable, it may be necessary to trim the top also.

The usual method of root pruning is to remove the tree from its pot and inspect the root ball. If it appears necessary to root prune then about one third of the soil is teased out from the sides and underside of the root ball to leave the exposed roots hanging freely; these are cut off carefully with scissors. The tree is then replanted in the same pot with fresh soil, tied into the pot if necessary to secure it, kept in shade and given extra attention until regeneration of the roots is well advanced.

The mineral particles that make up natural soils range from sand, the coarsest, to clay, the finest. Clay will retain water and sand will provide good drainage. The roots of plants require

FORMAL UPRIGHT JAPANESE LARCH
(Larix leptolepis)
In 1977 a spindly six year old seedling was rescued from a bonfire. It had a severe right-angle bend in the trunk and no useful branch structure. Nevertheless, eleven years of patient training and ingenuity have miraculously produced this 18 inch high formal upright.

both air and water and a good soil has a high percentage of air–water space in relation to its solid elements. An ideal soil in addition to having the structural porosity of sand and the water–retaining ability of clay, contains the right amount of decaying vegetable and other organic matter which we call humus. Such a soil will suit most bonsai, although too much clay will tend to compact the compost and clog the air spaces. The enthusiast can either make up his own or use as a base a proprietory compost. The Japanese sieve their potting soils, retaining several granular sizes but discarding very fine particles. They pot with dry soil. Dry soil can be tamped around the roots without destroying its granular structure but damp potting soil containing clay will lose much of its porosity if firmly packed into the pot.

When potting or repotting, the drainage hole or holes in the pot are covered with a porous material, such as plastic mesh, and a thin layer of coarse soil particles is spread over the base of the pot to ensure good drainage. Finer soil is worked into the roots until potting is satisfactorily completed. The top can then be dressed. Finally, the planting is thoroughly but gently watered. At a later stage moss or rocks may be added.

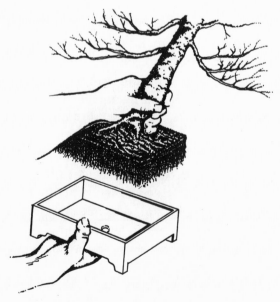

The roots of a bonsai may be examined by carefully easing the tree out of its pot. If it appears to be root-bound it is ready for repotting.

TWIN TRUNK STYLE TRIDENT MAPLE
(Acer buergerianum)
The immense eight inch thick trunk base and exaggerated taper give this 24 inch tall tree a masculine appearance. It took only 60 years to achieve this dramatic effect, which is why trident maples are so popular as material for bonsai.

OVERLEAF

RAFT STYLE TRIDENT MAPLE
(Acer buergerianum)
This tree was imported from Japan in 1968 and over the years much work has been carried out to improve and refine the shape. It is approximately 100 years old and stands 18 inches tall.

POTS

The pot of a bonsai is like the frame of a picture and it should be selected carefully to show the plant or plants to the best advantage. The pot must have adequate drainage and be made of a material which looks well and will withstand exposure to frost and weathering.

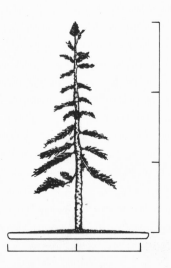

To create a visual balance the length of the pot should be two-thirds to three-quarters of the height of the tree.

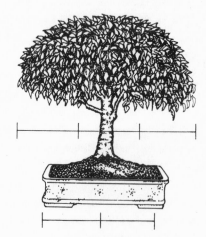

If the tree is low and spreading the pot should ideally be about three-quarters of the width of the tree. Avoid using a pot which has similar dimensions to either the height or the width of the bonsai.

INFORMAL UPRIGHT TRIDENT MAPLE
(Acer buergerianum)
This tree was imported as a stump in 1976. All the branches and twigs have been grown from scratch since then. The well-formed root flare and gnarled trunk give this 40 year old tree an air of great maturity.

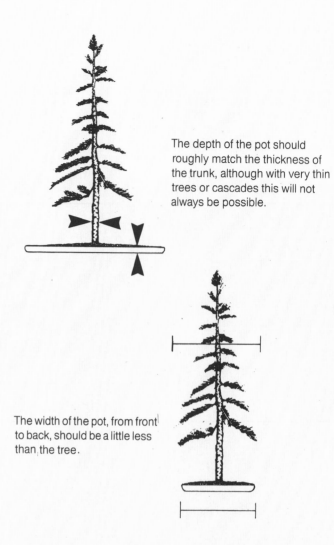

The depth of the pot should roughly match the thickness of the trunk, although with very thin trees or cascades this will not always be possible.

The width of the pot, from front to back, should be a little less than the tree.

立木

INFORMAL UPRIGHT JAPANESE MAPLE

(Acer palmatum)

Japanese maples are valued for their striking autumn colours as well as their delicate foliage. This 22 year old specimen was a nondescript branchless trunk when it was imported in 1977. Since then 12 inches have been added to the height and all the branches have grown on to produce a very graceful bonsai.

Shallow flower pots or seed trays make good training pots. When the training of a bonsai is sufficiently advanced, a pot is chosen in which to display it, the size and shape depending upon the size and shape of the tree. Upright trees show to advantage in oval or rectangular pots and are placed slightly off-centre. In a round or hexagonal pot the tree is best placed centrally. Heavy, deep pots suit a thick trunk and thick dark foliage whereas a tall and lightly framed tree requires a shallow and more delicate pot to show it to advantage.

Imported Japanese pots are becoming more expensive but local potters are making pots suitable for bonsai and the enthusiast can make his or her own, at least in the smaller sizes, at an evening class.

PETER CHAN

TRAINING AND MAINTENANCE

The training of a bonsai begins when it is strong enough and large enough to withstand treatment. With seedlings this is perhaps when the young tree has formed shoots about two inches long. With more mature trees it should not be undertaken until the tree is showing all the signs of good health. The beginning of training is seeing the tree's potential. It is essential to study the tree carefully and decide what size and shape it is to be, bearing in mind its species and natural form. It is very important to decide at the beginning which side of the tree is the 'front'.

There are a number of methods of training bonsai including pinching, trimming, pruning, wiring, tying and feeding. The principal methods of maintaining a trained tree in good order are pinching, trimming, leaf trimming and feeding.

Pinching and trimming
Shape is both created and maintained by pinching and trimming. Some new leaf buds are removed in spring, and to a degree throughout the growing season, to prevent the growth of unwanted shoots. Buds are encouraged to grow where, and to the extent that, new shoots are required. Trimming may be done with scissors or with the fingers. The greatest care must be taken to remove only what is not required. The precise methods of pinching and trimming, which vary from species to species, are illustrated.

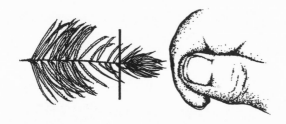

Trees with needle-like foliage, such as spruce or larch (but not pines) should have their shoots pinched back to about a quarter of their length. This is done while the shoots are still tender and before they have fully elongated.

INFORMAL UPRIGHT SCOTS PINE
(Pinus sylvestris)
This 32 inch tall pine was collected from the wild over ten years ago and is still undergoing training. In spite of this, its beautifully proportioned foliage masses and trunk line make it an extremely desirable tree. Its age is estimated to be 40 years.

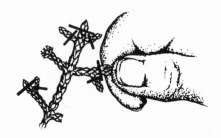

The shoots of trees with cord-like foliage, such as Chinese juniper, can be nipped hard back at almost any time during the growing season. Use the thumb and forefinger, and twist and pull at the same time. The shoot will break cleanly and easily.

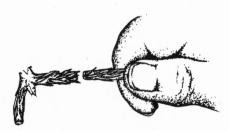

On pines the new shoots, or candles, can be nipped in the same way as above. This must be done as the candles elongate, just as the minute new needles begin to appear.

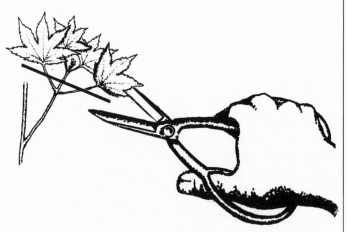

Deciduous trees respond well to having the terminal buds removed together with the top one or two sets of leaves. Always use sharp scissors.

Pruning

Once they are mature, pines dislike drastic pruning. Most other trees, however, will survive very drastic pruning and dormant buds can be encouraged to break to produce new branches in the desired place.

INFORMAL STYLE HAWTHORN
(Crataegus monogyna)
This 36 inch tall specimen was rescued from a condemned hedgerow and was carefully nurtured back to health before styling took place. What is now the trunk was originally a hanging branch, the whole tree has been tilted by about 100 degrees to achieve the desired angle. In fact the trunk sweeps dramatically forwards, which prompted its creator, Dan Barton, to name it 'Ascending Crane'. It is impossible to estimate its age accurately but it must be well over 70 years old.

Wiring

The best wire to use is copper or aluminium, although plastic-coated iron wire is also suitable. Wires of different thickness are used according to the size of the branch or trunk. The aim is to wind a spiral of wire on to the branch so that the wire and the branch can be bent together to the desired shape. However great caution is required and the newcomer to training bonsai would be well advised to practise on unwanted branches first.

Wire should be applied to the branch or trunk sufficiently tightly to be in contact with the bark, but never so tight that it digs in. The illustration on the left shows wire applied at too shallow an angle — this could restrict the flow of sap and has little holding power. The centre illustration shows wire applied too loosely, which would have absolutely no holding power at all. The wire on the right has been applied correctly — a 45 degree angle is about right.

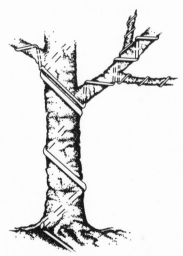

Several different thicknesses of wire can be used to hold branches of different weights. Wires on the trunk should be anchored in the soil. Wire on branches should be firmly anchored around another branch or used to shape an adjacent branch. Always run wires parallel to each other, never allow wires to cross since this will create pressure points which will damage the bark.

石上樹

ROOT-OVER-ROCK STYLE BLAAUW'S JUNIPER
(Juniperus x media 'Blaauw')
A rooted cutting was planted directly over the rock 16 years ago and left to grow unchecked for eight years in order to establish the root structure. Only then did the training of the branches begin. The height including the rock is now 17 inches.

Tying

It is possible, and very interesting, to train a tree without wiring it. A tie may be attached to a branch which can then be pulled in the desired direction and the other end of the tie fixed to the container or to another suitable anchorage. Alternatively a weight may be suspended from the tie. Ties must not be allowed to cut into the bark and should be removed as soon as the branch has set in its new position.

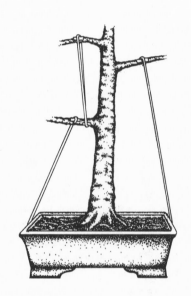

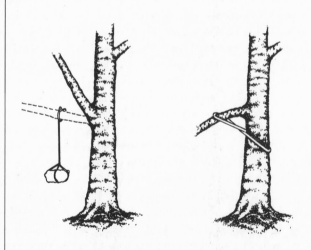

Various methods of tying can be used to pull the branches into the desired position, however none of them is as accurate as wiring. Of all the methods illustrated, the suspended weight method is probably the least effective.

FORMAL UPRIGHT STYLE CRYPTOMERIA

(Cryptomeria japonica)
This classically-styled cryptomeria was estimated to be 50 years old when it was imported in 1976. The well-formed root flare and trunk taper combine with the carefully placed branches to create an almost perfect example of the formal upright style.

PETER ADAMS

Feeding

Successful training and maintenance depend upon having a healthy tree. Both too much and too little food will have undesirable results. A feeding programme is shown within the work schedule.

Leaf trimming

Certain deciduous trees, notably the maples, benefit when healthy from having all their leaves cut off during late spring or early summer. The new crop of leaves will be smaller and more beautiful. Five-needle pines react to having the still soft new needles pulled out in the spring by producing the following spring very short, bunched needles which enhance the beauty of this type of bonsai. However this should only be done about every three or four years.

Work schedule

The work schedule which follows has been designed for use in both northern and southern hemispheres. As in all gardening the work is seasonal and the precise timing of various operations will depend upon the climate, altitude and latitude of the reader's garden and the schedule can be adapted accordingly.

DRIFTWOOD STYLE CHINESE JUNIPER
(Juniperus chinensis)
This massive 35 inch tall specimen was imported from Japan in 1970, and was said to be over 100 years old at the time. It is thought that this tree was formed by splitting the trunk away from its parent tree, which would explain the shari (exposed heartwood) on both front and back of the trunk. The abrupt change in direction of the trunk is perfectly countered by the shape and weight of the foliage masses.

PETER ADAMS

BROOM STYLE ENGLISH ELM
(Ulmus procera)
At only eight inches tall this tiny tree has
been developed to resemble a semi-
mature tree in a parkland setting. It took
fourteen years of intricate pinching of new
shoots to achieve this result.

APPRECIATION AND JUDGEMENT

For those who have possessed bonsai for a con-
siderable time, whether by purchase or by the
creation of their own specimens, there is little or
no difficulty in seeing at once the good or bad
qualities of a tree which they are examining for
the first time.

A newcomer to the art, however, may not
always know what to look for.

Locally grown trees are occasionally offered
for sale, but, as a rule, such trees are at best good
raw material on which future training may be
carried out. If an imported tree is under consid-
eration, other factors come into play.

At the top of the scale there are of course the
masterpieces with few, if any, defects. There are
also many imported trees which, while superfi-
cially satisfactory, reveal faults on close inspec-
tion and which will entail a great deal of work
before they can be regarded as really good examples of bonsai.

This does not mean to say that such lower
grade trees are not worth having. The trunk and
pot may be good, for example, and the head
capable of improvement, but one must be aware
of what one is acquiring or judging.

There will probably be many shortcomings to
see in any tree in its early stages of development,
but at the same time one must not be unduly
impressed by the aged appearance of a tree to
the exclusion of all other aesthetic considera-
tions. It is surprising, in the light of the counsels
of perfection offered in expert writings on the
subject, how many unhealed wounds or scars
from wiring (and even wire left on too long) can
be seen on otherwise reasonably good imported
trees. Such blemishes should count against a tree
when exhibited in a show, for at such a moment
the tricks and scars of training should, ideally, be
invisible.

Every tree has its best side from which it is

meant to be viewed. It is perhaps legitimate, if undesirable, for the unseen side to have certain blemishes; but from the front, branches must appear to spring naturally from the trunk or from larger branches, and must never sprout brush-like from a branch which has been cut straight across without any regard for an appearance of natural development.

Presentation and display 'en masse' can cover a multitude of sins, but a bonsai is intended to stand or fall on its individual merits or demerits. The satisfactory relation of the tree to its pot is of the first importance, and after that comes the setting in which the bonsai is placed for exhibition.

The following points may be of help to those judging bonsai, as well as to owners wishing to exhibit at shows.

GOOD

1. A strong, well shaped trunk, tapering upwards, springing naturally from the soil.

2. A good fanning out of surface roots from the base of the trunk, gradually disappearing into the soil.

3. A good, well proportioned head of branches which are well spaced and set naturally on the trunk.

4. The tree as natural looking as possible in the context of the idiom.

5. The pot itself, preferably in monochrome glazes, must be in proportion to the tree, to form an artistic unity. Decorated polychrome pots can of course be used but look wrong when containing flowering or fruiting trees.

6. The tree should be placed in the pot so as to create a visual balance. For example, if the base of the trunk is towards the right-hand edge, the main weight of the head should incline leftwards.

7. Flowers or fruit, on varieties which are grown to produce these, must be in proportion, for

DRIFTWOOD STYLE NEEDLE JUNIPER
(Juniperus rigida)
Said to be 130 years old when imported in 1974, this magnificent tree shows all the signs of generations of styling and refinement. At 24 inches tall, the well-proportioned crown is in perfect balance with the ancient driftwood trunk.

INFORMAL UPRIGHT TRIDENT MAPLE

(Acer buergerianum)
When it was imported in 1973 this tree was nothing but a stump of a trunk with no branches at all. It was then about 25 years old and 13 inches tall. Over the years, however, new branches and a new leader were grown on until the present design was achieved. The current height of the tree is 30 inches.

example a full sized apple would look absurd on a tree one or two feet high.

8. If large leafed trees are used, fewer branches are best, so that the general effect is of an 'impressionist' order, with each leaf giving a broad sweep of green. Pinnate leaves, of course, give an illusion of a branch bearing small leaves.

9. A tree growing with its roots clasping a rock must really adhere and not merely be wrapped loosely round.

10. A tree should be planted well raised up in its pot, so that the bole can be clearly seen if viewed at eye level over the rim of the pot.

11. Stones and moss or other covering of the surface of the soil must look natural and well established.

12. If deciduous trees are shown in winter, invisibility of scars and marks of training is of paramount importance.

BAD

1. A weak, badly shaped trunk, or one which looks as though it were merely a branch stuck in the soil.

2. Badly spaced or crossed branches, or those rubbing one on another.

3. Badly cut branches that have in no way callused over.

4. Elaborately artificial effects, often caused by wiring into unnatural curves.

5. Snagged and abruptly cut roots visible above the soil, or dead fibrous roots standing up in the air.

6. A tree placed exaggeratedly out of balance.

7. Flowers or fruit out of proportion to the size of tree.

8. A pot which is out of harmony with its tree. For example a decorated polychrome pot used

for flowering or fruiting species. Plastic pots are aesthetically bad.

9. Foliage which totally hides the trunk, giving the appearance of a bush instead of a tree.

10. A tree planted with the soil and bole sunk far below the rim of its container.

11. Untidy surface of the soil, and fussy, unnecessary decoration such as ill-shaped, unnatural looking stones.

12. A tree grown in a style totally alien to its species.

LITERATI STYLE JAPANESE BLACK PINE
(Pinus thunbergii)
When this tree was imported in 1970 it was described as 'a flat topped bush' but its owner soon restyled it by wiring down the branches and creating the jin on the lower right hand side. At 30 inches tall and 38 years old it is now a much improved and highly desirable bonsai.

寄植

GROUP STYLE JAPANESE LARCH

(Larix leptolepis)

This 33 inch tall group is composed entirely of seedlings sown at the same time in 1968. The apparent difference in ages has been achieved by allowing some trees to grow vigorously for a few years while restricting the growth of others. Note how the smaller trees have been planted towards the rear to give greater perspective.

PETER ADAMS

SEASONAL WORK SCHEDULE

Readers are requested to note that in order to make the text intelligible in both hemispheres, plant flowering times etc are generally described in terms of seasons, not months. The following table provides an approximate 'translation' of seasons into months for the two hemispheres.

Northern hemisphere		Southern hemisphere
Mid-winter	January	Mid-summer
Late winter	February	Late summer
Early spring	March	Early autumn
Mid-spring	April	Mid-autumn
Late spring	May	Late autumn
Early summer	June	Early winter
Mid-summer	July	Mid-winter
Late summer	August	Late winter
Early autumn	September	Early spring
Mid-autumn	October	Mid-spring
Late autumn	November	Late spring
Early winter	December	Early summer

MID-WINTER

Watering
As for early winter. See note below under 'General'.

Repotting
Do not repot.

Feeding
Do not feed.

Pruning
Do not prune.

Trimming
As for mid-autumn.

直幹

FORMAL STYLE JAPANESE MAPLE

(Acer palmatum 'Kashima')
This 27 inch tall dwarf variety of Japanese maple was imported in 1981 and was said to be 35 years old at that time. Its unusual lower branch structure and its massive 33 inch spread make this a very desirable specimen.

Root pruning
Do not root prune.

Insect pests
These should already have been eliminated.

Wiring
Leave it alone.

Propagation
Cuttings. For seeds, see mid-autumn.

General
Inspect periodically, especially when snow may start to fall. The greatest danger is drought due to a snow-covered pot drying out. Perhaps the best antidote is to put the pot in the bath and spray with cold water until the snow is dispersed. The temperature should be kept low, but the water will get to the soil eventually. Keep in a cool room or put outside during the day in sunshine if possible. If you have ordered loam, peat and other supplies, start getting them ready.

LATE WINTER

Watering
In dry weather, twice a week. In wet weather, let the rain do it for you, but give water if it has not rained for three days. Water in the morning.

Repotting
No repotting this month. Make sure you have plenty of dry sifted soil ingredients or compost ready for the spring, and store under cover. If you have not already done so, make a list of the trees you intend to re-pot. To decide if this is needed, turn the root ball out of its container carefully and examine it; if it is a tight network of roots then it needs root pruning and repotting. This is done to keep the roots active and growing in fresh new soil. Check that you have all reserve pots cleaned ready for potting on.

Feeding
Hardly necessary yet. For trees that are not to be

INFORMAL UPRIGHT JAPANESE HORNBEAM
(Carpinus laxiflora)
This 18 inch tall tree is surprisingly well proportioned for its 15 years. The delicate foliage turns yellow, then golden brown in autumn, and remains on the tree all winter.

INFORMAL UPRIGHT SCOTS PINE

(Pinus sylvestris var. *beuvronensis)*
In 1974 this tree was bought from a nursery as an eight year old garden plant. Its naturally dwarf habit and tight foliage make it an ideal variety for bonsai. It took only 14 years to produce this 32 inch tall, very mature looking specimen, which could compete on equal terms with any Japanese white pine.

DRIFTWOOD STYLE SLOE
(Prunus spinosa)
This tree was considerably larger than its current 14 inches when it was originally collected from a condemned hedgerow, but it was drastically pruned to a limbless trunk and all the branches were grown on from scratch. The striking shari (exposed heartwood) was created later. This free-flowering species is uncommon as a bonsai, a fact which does not do it justice.

石
付

ROOT-ON-ROCK STYLE SLOE
(Prunus spinosa)
This collected tree was first planted on the
rock in 1977 and has remained there
undisturbed for the last 12 years. Every
spring this tiny nine inch tall tree produces
masses of fragrant white flowers.

雙樹

TWIN TRUNK JAPANESE HORNBEAM
(Carpinus laxiflora)
Originally this tree had three trunks, but after importing it in 1975 Peter Adams removed the central one and converted the design to a more pleasing and better balanced twin trunk. The scar, where the middle trunk used to be, has been hollowed out over the years and is now an integral part of the tree, adding character and age. At 55 years old, this tree is now 28 inches tall.

repotted, but where plenty of future growth is desired, a little bone meal can be given.

Pruning
It is not advisable to remove unwanted branches or twigs yet. Those that you remove may be alive, those that you leave may turn out to be dead.

Trimming
None is necessary yet.

Root pruning
Not yet.

Insect pests
Still too early to worry, except for citrus, which may have brown scale insects still undetected. Pick these off by hand.

Wiring
Not yet.

Propagation
Prepare seedpans for sowing. Soak slow-starting seeds and sow under glass. A good month to start striking willow cuttings.

General
In cold weather keep tender plants in an unheated room. Water them once a week. Check all pots for cracks or frost damage and trees for gale damage, and add casualties to repotting list. Check condition of tools, sieves, syringe and other apparatus. Watch for movement in early flowering trees such as *chaenomeles*, forsythia, winter jasmine.

EARLY SPRING

Watering
As for late winter, spray any repotted trees daily.

Repotting
Have you followed the late winter instruction? Make sure now and remedy deficiencies. Watch the buds of trees listed for repotting. Mild weather may bring them on. As soon as they

PETER ADAMS

start to move, repot quickly, and shelter them from wind. Cold weather later in the month may be drying and cause checks. Root prune when you are repotting.

Feeding
As for late winter. Do not feed newly repotted trees.

Pruning
Unwanted branches may be removed only if the retained branches are clearly alive with buds on the move. But exercise restraint. Prune back to a suitable live bud pointing in the right direction. Seal large wounds with a sealing compound.

Trimming
Where too much growth is expected, and buds are well advanced, removal of unwanted future twigs may be anticipated by pinching out buds now. Where bushiness is desired, terminal buds may be pinched out if they are adequately supported by numerous lower buds. But do not overdo pinching.

Root pruning
See above under 'Repotting'.

Insect pests
Still too early, but see late winter note.

Wiring
Not yet. Remove any existing wire that might cut into the bark.

Propagation
Sow any seeds you left out last month. Suggestions for early spring sowing are Maule's dwarf quince, cedar, pine, crab, *punica granatum nana*, cypress, *sophora japonica*. Take softwood cuttings when buds are well on the move.

General
Check stock of insecticides, fertilisers, wire. Inspect unopened buds for signs of opening. Wash down all storage shelves and benches and outside of all pots. Glazed pots of Japanese origin can be cleaned by rubbing down with scouring powder, or if dirt is extremely hard to dislodge, with steel wool. Examine apparently dead

GROUP STYLE BLAAUW'S JUNIPER
(Juniperus x media 'Blaauw')
Composed of trees ranging from ten to 20 years old, this group was styled by John Naka of California using commercial nursery stock. The tallest tree in the group is 32 inches high.

trees, but do not discard such casualties yet. Add new top soil where required to trees not being repotted. Many may require this after winter rains. In others the top soil may look sour; remove this and replace with fresh compost.

MID-SPRING

Watering
Give water once a day if it does not rain, sparingly for older trees, more for young trees where growth is wanted. Spray repotted trees daily.

Repotting
Complete all repotting.

Feeding
Do not feed trees repotted this month. Feed sparingly any trees repotted more than two weeks ago. Feed flowering trees which have not been repotted. Others may have bone meal mixed with a little wood ash and dried blood.

Pruning
As for early spring, but you can be bolder if the buds are breaking.

Trimming
As for early spring, but pinching can be resorted to more boldly.

Root pruning
Root prune as necessary all trees being repotted. Trees not being repotted can be lifted out and roots inspected, but do not prune if they show healthy new white ends and are not becoming root-bound. Trim off any roots that have grown out through the drainage holes.

Insect pests
Watch for red spider and white scale. Spray with insecticide at appropriate strength.

Wiring
Not yet. Have you removed all dangerous existing wiring? (See early spring note.)

INFORMAL STYLE ENGLISH OAK
(Quercus robur)
This unique oak tree was first dug up from a garden in 1957, when it was estimated to be 20 years old. It was immediately planted in a half barrel, where it remained undisturbed until 1980, at which point its creator, Harry Tomlinson, persuaded the owner to part with it. After only six years training it was exhibited at the national exhibition in Osaka, Japan, where it won a first prize. It is unquestionably the finest example of a bonsai oak in existence.

INFORMAL UPRIGHT RED MAPLE

(*Acer palmatum* 'Beni Seigai')
This incredibly beautiful 34 inch tall tree was imported from Japan in 1976 and is now over 100 years old. The transition of the foliage colour from pink in spring, through delicate greens to vivid red in autumn is in itself enough to make this tree the star of any collection.

Propagation

Take cuttings of late starters. Pot on last year's seedlings.

General

Remove weeds. Plant moss. Inspect unopened buds for signs of opening. Be ready to give protection against night frosts to trees with newly-opened leaves. Consider discarding winter casualties. If flowering bonsai are brought indoors for display, they should be kept away from any source of heat and should not be kept indoors for more than a couple of days at a time.

LATE SPRING

Watering

As for mid-spring. On warm days water twice daily any tree whose growth is to be encouraged. Spray repotted trees daily.

Repotting

It is really almost too late to re-pot, so do it early and do it quickly if you must.

Feeding

Solids can be given every ten days if growth is to be encouraged. A little liquid feed diluted to half strength can also be added to the water once a week. Generous feeding for flowering trees, and for deciduous trees that have been leaf-cut.

Pruning

Young trees under training – remove any remaining unwanted branches. Older trees – check that the wounds where any branches have been removed are carved and shaped to permit the callus to grow over them.

Trimming

Keep a constant check to pinch unwanted buds and new shoots. Leaf-cut deciduous trees if you wish to increase twigginess, provided the leaves have become 'leather-hard'.

石上樹

ROOT-OVER-ROCK STYLE
TRIDENT MAPLE
(Acer buergerianum)
Since its importation in the early 1970s the entire branch structure has been regrown to create this classic 20 inch high specimen. The way the heavy roots hug the rock, and the ease with which a compact rugged tree-form can be produced explains why trident maple is so frequently chosen for this style.

DAN BARTON

74

Root pruning
See mid-spring note for trees that have not been repotted.

Insect pests
Watch for red spider, aphids, ants, mealy bugs. Spray. Cut off infected leaves of deciduous trees and burn them.

Wiring
Start on the larger branches.

Propagation
Conifer cuttings.

General
Remove weeds. Put sun-sensitive trees such as elms and zelkovas into half shade, but still be ready with frost protection (see mid-spring note) for newly opened trees. Inspect unopened buds for signs of opening.

EARLY SUMMER

Watering
Water morning and evening every day in dry weather.

Repotting
Too late for potting in new soil, which would disturb roots, but you can pot on if you are careful to leave the old soil ball undisturbed.

Feeding
As for late spring.

Pruning
As for late spring.

Trimming
As for late spring. Check daily if possible.

Root pruning
Avoid this.

Insect pests
As for late spring. Try to check every day.

Wiring
Wire smaller branches.

立木

INFORMAL STYLE TRIDENT MAPLE

(Acer buergerianum)
This massive 34 inch tall tree was imported in 1968 at a reputed age of 90 years. The gentle curve of the trunk and well separated foliage masses create an elegance which is unusual in this species.

石上樹

ROOT-OVER-ROCK STYLE PYRACANTHA
(Pyracantha angustifolia)
Including the rock, this gorgeous tree stands 24 inches tall and was produced in 35 years. Pyracantha is not only a common garden shrub, but also makes spectacular bonsai. Tiny white flowers in early summer are followed by brilliant red or orange berries which persist on the plant all winter. This photograph was taken in early spring when there was still enough fruit to weigh down the branches.

Propagation
If this season's seedlings are thriving, pot on into small training pots.

General
Remove weeds, especially liverwort if it is rampant. Keep sun-sensitive trees in half shade.

MID-SUMMER

Watering
Water and spray foliage morning and evening every day, except when appreciable rain has fallen. Avoid watering in direct sunlight if possible. Be generous to trees planted in shallow pots, trees with a lot of moss in their pots, and trees subject to drying wind.

Repotting
Do not re-pot. If a pot is broken or the soil is partially washed out by heavy rain, or disturbed by animals or accidents, pack the soil ball into a new pot without disturbing the roots.

Feeding
Give occasional feeds. Little and often is better than large amounts. Feed more generously trees undergoing heavy trimming or leaf-cutting.

Pruning
Pruning can still be carried out.

Trimming
Growth is still fairly rapid in many trees. Maple, zelkova, elm, must be constantly trimmed. Spruce and juniper may still need their new needles shortened by pinching. Check each tree daily if possible. Remove dead brown needles from conifers.

Root pruning
Avoid this.

Insect pests
Try to check every day. Cut off infected leaves. Spray.

PETER CHAN

Wiring
Do not wire.

Propagation
Cuttings can always be taken.

General
Remove weeds, especially liverwort. Keep sun-sensitive trees in half shade – maple, elm, japonica and any that show signs of leaf scorch.

LATE SUMMER

Watering
As for mid-summer.

Repotting
As for mid-summer.

Feeding
Begin to taper off the feeding. Stop solids but continue with a little liquid feed in the watering.

Pruning
Avoid pruning if possible.

Trimming
Little is now needed, as growth will have slowed down. Remove dead brown needles from conifers.

Root pruning
Avoid this, except for fast root-growers, such as willow, cherry, chestnut, ash. Lift the soil ball out of the pot and examine, but do not prune unless the bottom surface is a solid mat of roots.

Insect pests
As for mid-summer.

Wiring
Do not wire.

Propagation
Take semi-hardwood cuttings for rooting under glass. This is a good month for any cuttings.

General
Keep down weeds. Sun-sensitive trees still need protection.

DRIFTWOOD STYLE JUNIPER
(Juniperus chinensis 'San Jose')
Originally grown as an ornamental garden plant, this tree was excavated in 1982 when it had grown to a spread of eight feet. After allowing it to live in a large flower pot for a few years, to establish a new root system, it was pruned and styled. The prominent driftwood areas reveal where the major branches were removed, but skilful shaping simulates the ravages of a harsh climate and immediately gives the tree an ancient appearance.

GROUP STYLE JAPANESE BEECH
(Fagus crenata)
At 36 inches high this group is taller than it seems in the photograph. The most attractive features of this species include the strikingly white bark on older trunks and the fact that it tends to retain its copper-coloured leaves all winter.

EARLY AUTUMN

Watering
Water at least once a day in dry weather.

Repotting
Those who favour autumn repotting for conifers could start late in the month.

Feeding
Feed very sparingly.

Pruning
Do not prune.

Trimming
There may be a pre-autumn burst of growth requiring light trimming.

Root pruning
Do not root prune.

Insect pests
As for mid-summer.

Wiring
Do not wire. Test wired branches gingerly to see if they have taken the required permanent set. If so, remove wire. Do not bend or rewire.

Propagation
Take semi-hardwood and hardwood cuttings.

General
Remove weeds and any moss not in top condition. Protect moss from birds, which at this time are searching for insects. Remove dead leaves and tidy up the pots. By now you may have found some wild trees for lifting. When possible, leave them for lifting next spring, but if this is not practicable, lift them now.

MID-AUTUMN

Watering
Water only in dry spells but check frequently.

Repotting
See early autumn note on repotting.

寄
植

GROUP STYLE ENGLISH ELM

(Ulmus procera)
The oldest tree in this group is seven years
old, the youngest only four. The planting
was assembled three years ago, each tree
having been pre-trained and shaped
specifically for the purpose. The tallest
tree is 13 inches high.

Feeding
Do not feed.

Pruning
Do not prune.

Trimming
Deciduous trees probably have no leaves to trim. Conifers should not be trimmed.

Root pruning
Do not root prune.

Insect pests
As for mid-summer, but there will not be many pests still active.

Wiring
As for early autumn.

Propagation
Cuttings as for early autumn. Plan your seed sowing programme. Probably the best overall results are obtained by gathering fresh seeds now and sowing for germination next spring. Hard coated seeds such as hawthorn may require up to 18 months stratification. If you have enough, divide seed into two batches, one for immediate sowing, the other for stratification.

General
As for early autumn. If you contemplate plunging any pots, get the ground ready now. If you are going to winter any pots inside, get suitable space cleared for them in a cool room. Most trees can stay outside but tender or exotic ones may need protection, as may conifers that would offer lodgment for snow.

LATE AUTUMN

Watering
Water sparingly.

Repotting
Do not re-pot.

Feeding
Do not feed.

Pruning
Do not prune.

Trimming
As for mid-autumn.

Root pruning
Do not root prune.

Insect pests
Check over all branches and twigs, and pick off any galls, blisters, scale insects and other infestations that may think they are settled in their winter quarters. Water thoroughly all trees, soil and pots with a mild disinfectant fungicide.

Wiring
As for early autumn.

Propagation
Cuttings. You can pot on last spring's seedlings if you do not disturb the root ball. This will save

BROOM STYLE JAPANESE MAPLE

(Acer palmatum 'Kashima')
The leaves on this dwarf variety of maple are among the earliest to emerge in spring. This photograph was taken in late winter and already the buds have burst and the young, bronze coloured foliage is beginning to show. Imported in 1986 by Peter Chan, it is said to be 65 years old and stands 20 inches high with a spread of 26 inches.

time next spring, when you are bound to be busy.

General
Review the trees that are to be given shelter – citrus, azaleas, conifers with spreading branches. Plunge or protect with straw. Gravel or cinders can be used to plunge the pots in. Check all pots to ensure that drainage holes are clear. Frosts are more dangerous to pots than to trees.

EARLY WINTER

Watering
Water only when necessary, keeping compost slightly on the dry side. Water in the morning, not the evening. It is inadvisable to have the pot full of water when the night temperature drop occurs.

Repotting
Do not re-pot.

Feeding
Do not feed.

Pruning
Do not prune.

Trimming
Do not trim.

Root pruning
Do not root prune.

Insect pests
As for late autumn if you have the energy.

Wiring
Leave it alone.

Propagation
Cuttings. For seeds, see mid-autumn.

General
Inspect periodically. If a pot is cracked, tie it up with string or the like as a temporary measure. It is not too early to check your supplies and order as necessary.

INDEX

Italic numerals refer to picture captions